Beers, V. Gilbert
Honeyphants and Elebees. Illustrated by Juel Krisvoy. Chicago, Moody Press, 1974.
unp. col.illus.

I.Krisvoy, Juel, illus. II.Title.

A WORD TO PARENTS AND TEACHERS

Have you ever wanted to be someone you're not? Or have you dreamed of doing things you can't? Most of us have. Children dream these dreams. So did Elmo Elephant and Miss Honi Bee in this story.

But strange things happen when Miss Honi becomes an elebee, and Elmo becomes a honeyphant. Things do not work out the way they planned. Of course, that's what happens when we try to be something we're not.

It's good to know that God has a plan for each of us. He made elephants to be elephants, and honeybees to be honeybees. He made you to be YOU, and He made your child in His own way.

Aren't you glad God made you and your child the way He did? You could be elephants, you know!

Honeyphants and Elebees

By V. Gilbert Beers

Illustrated by Juel Krisvoy

©1974 by
V. Gilbert Beers
Library of Congress Catalog Number: 73-20886
ISBN: 0-8024-3612-9
Printed in the United States of America

Moody Press

Chicago

Will you come to the zoo?
Will you come there with me
To a hole in the side
Of an old hollow tree?
It's Miss Honi Bee's home,
Filled with sweet honeycomb,
It is just the right place
For Miss Honi to be.

By the old hollow tree
There's a fence that is high.
When you stand on a stump,
It's as high as your eye.
That's where Big Elmo spends
All his time with his friends,
Eating good peanut treats
That your friends and you buy.

On a warm summer day
When you've nothing to do,
You may stay by the fence
And your friends may stay, too.
If you look up ahead
At the bright flower bed,
You may see Honi Bee
Making honey for you.

You may watch Honi Bee
For a minute or two,
But there's someone, you think,
Who is more fun for you.
It's Big Elmo you chose,
With his funny big nose,
And the things that you like
To see elephants do.

When you've gone from the zoo,
And your friends are away,
Would you like to know what
These two neighbors might say?
Don't you wish that you knew
What these two neighbors do
As they meet at the fence
On a bright summer day?

Would you think that it's strange
If Miss Honi would say,
"All the children come here
To see you every day.
Do you think that they care
That I tear out my hair
Making honey for them,
While you're eating your hay?"

But the elephant said,
"I am such a disgrace!
Do you think it is fun
Just to stand in this place?
I would rather go fly
To a cloud in the sky,
Than have people stand here
And make fun of my face."

"Yes, the life that you live
Is the right life for me.
That's why I want to fly
From this pen and be free,"
The big elephant said,
With a toss of his head.
"I must leave this old pen.
I don't want to be me."

So Miss Honi Bee buzzed
And she gave a long sigh,
"Have you ever been chased
By a big dragonfly?
When that ugly bird flew,
Did he try to eat you?
Those are things you will find
When you fly in the sky."

"Don't you know that folks run
From each bee that they see?
Don't you know that they swat
When they think that it's me?
Don't you know that they mash
And they spray and they smash
Anything they can find
That they think is a bee?"

Then Miss Honi Bee said,
"Here are things you can do.
You can do funny tricks
At the circus or zoo.
You can lead a parade
Or just stand in the shade.
Do you see why I want
To be someone like you?"

WHAT DO YOU KNOW ABOUT ELEPHANTS?

1. Is an elephant the biggest animal in the zoo?
   (a) yes   (b) no

2. How many bees does it take to weigh as much as an elephant?
   (a) 5,000   (b) 50,000   (c) 50 million

3. How fast can an elephant run?
   (a) 5 miles per hour   (b) 25 miles per hour

4. How much can an elephant lift?
   (a) 6 pounds   (b) 600   (c) 6,000

5. What are an elephant's tusks made of?
   (a) pearl   (b) ivory   (c) marble

6. How big can an elephant's ears grow?
   (a) 4 inches   (b) 4 feet   (c) 40 feet

7. How thick is an elephant's skin?
   (a) 1/4 inch   (b) 1 inch   (c) 1 foot

8. How long can an elephant live?
   (a) 6 years   (b) 16 years   (c) 60 years

9. How long can an elephant's tusks grow?
   (a) 8 inches   (b) 8 feet

10. Who can make an elephant?
    (a) you   (b) God   (c) a zookeeper

Answers: 1a, 2c, 3b, 4b, 5b, 6b, 7b, 8c, 9b, 10b.

"Who can fly in the sky
And still live at the zoo?"
The big elephant asked.
"Who can make honey, too?
Let me ask in a quiz
What a honeybee is.
Then you'll know why I want
To be someone like you."

WHAT DO YOU KNOW ABOUT HONEYBEES?

1. How far do honeybees fly to get a pound of honey?
   (a) around the block   (b) around the world

2. Do honeybees die after they sting?
   (a) yes   (b) no

3. Can honey help athletes do their work better?
   (a) yes   (b) no

4. How strong is a drop of honeybee sting? As strong as
   (a) a drop of alcohol   (b) a drop of rattlesnake poison

5. How long does it take a honeybee to wear out her wings?
   (a) 6 weeks   (b) 6 months   (c) 6 years

6. How many honeybees will you often find in a hive?
   (a) 500   (b) 5,000   (c) 50,000

7. What do honeybees eat?
   (a) flowers   (b) wax   (c) honey

8. Which kind of honeybees make honey?
   (a) girls   (b) boys   (c) both

9. What kind of work can a honeybee do?
   (a) make wax   (b) make glue   (c) guard her honey

10. What else can a honeybee do?
    (a) heat and cool her house   (b) take out her garbage

Answers: 1b, 2a, 3a, 4b, 5a, 6c, 7c, 8a, 9a,b,c, 10a,b.

Then the two neighbors changed.
They are different, you see.
Can you find Honi now?
She's a big elebee.
But an elebee's sting
Is a thing with some zing!
So you'd better not sit
On an elebee's knee.

If you think that you see
Little elephants fly,
Just remember who said
That he wanted to try.
Those are honeyphants there,
And they don't have a care,
As they zoom through the zoo
And they fly through the sky.

But the elebees can't
Learn to play very well.
They're as busy as bees,
You can certainly tell.
Do you think that today
They'll make honey from hay?
Or a honeycomb home
From a small peanut shell?

Do you like a parade
On a bright summer day?
When the elebees buzz,
The parade runs away.
"We could get some bad stings,
If we stay with those things,"
All the animals said.
"We would rather go play."

Then the honeyphants said,
"It is time to have fun."
So the zookeeper knew
It was time that he run.
But when he flew around
With a net that he found,
All the honeyphants knew
That the zoo man had won.

Now the honeyphants thought
They would try something new,
So they filled up their trunks
With some honey and blew!
But then honey's to eat,
In your taster it's sweet.
In your pockets and hair
You will find it's like glue.

Would you like to come back
With your friends here today?
If you could, you might hear
What the elebees say.
"We are tired of this pen,
And we don't have a friend.
We just want to fly up
From these peanuts and hay."

Have you seen such a mess
As that honeyphant goo?
Do you think that you know
What those poor things should do?
They are longing today
For a small wisp of hay.
They are wishing that they
Could have peanuts from you.

What would YOU like to say
To your friends at the zoo?
Would you like to tell each,
"Why don't YOU please be YOU?"
Do you think you would say,
"God made you in His way.
You'll do best if you try
What He wants you to do?"

So the next time you come
To the fence at the zoo,
You will find Honi Bee
And Big Elmo there, too.
They are happy they can
Do the things in God's plan,
And they'll tell you right now,
"Why don't YOU please be YOU?"

SOMETHING TO TALK ABOUT

1. Who made you the way you are? What is wrong with trying to be someone you are not? Can you ever be someone else? Why do you think God wants you to be you? Why do you think He wants you to do the very best with yourself that you can?

2. Why do you think it is not always best to be biggest, or fastest, or strongest, or prettiest? What did the elebees learn? What did the honeyphants learn? What did you learn about you from these two?

3. Which can make the best honey, elephants or honeybees? Which can do the best tricks at a circus? Which is bigger? Which one can sting? Why didn't God make us all exactly alike? Why did He make you so that you can do some things your friends can't do? Why did He make your friends so that they can do some things you can't do?

4. What are some lessons you learned from honeybees and elephants? Which one gives its life to save others? Jesus did that, too, didn't He? Which one makes life sweeter for others by the work she does? Do you want to make the lives of others sweeter, too? How can you do that? Which one is the most fun to be near? Are you fun to be near, too?

5. Be glad God made you to be you. Try to find out what you can do best. Then do your very best for God and others.